He was Born For me : An April Fool's Tale

He was Born For Me
An April Fool's Tale

ANGELICA A. OLIVARES

ReadersMagnet, LLC

He was Born For Me : An April Fool's Tale
Copyright © 2024 by Angelica A. Olivares

Published in the United States of America

Library of Congress Control Number: 2024902646
ISBN   Paperback: 979-8-89091-455-2
ISBN   eBook: 979-8-89091-456-9

All rights reserved. No part of this publication may be reproduced, stored in a retrieval system or transmitted in any way by any means, electronic, mechanical, photocopy, recording or otherwise without the prior permission of the author except as provided by USA copyright law.

The opinions expressed by the author are not necessarily those of ReadersMagnet, LLC.

ReadersMagnet, LLC
10620 Treena Street, Suite 230 | San Diego, California, 92131 USA
1.619. 354. 2643 | www.readersmagnet.com

Book design copyright © 2024 by ReadersMagnet, LLC. All rights reserved.

Cover design by Ericka Obando
Interior design by Dorothy Lee

DEDICATION

I dedicate this little book to my mom, Teresa Mama; she has always been my husband's hero, because he says she is the one who convinced me that he was the man for me, who would make me happy the rest of my life. It's absolutely true. She did tell me many times that summer in 1970, that he was born for me. You were right, Teresa Mama.

CHAPTER 1

As an adolescent, I had severe depression; I felt so lonely. My days were routine and gray. I went through life feeling like a robot, and just surviving. I did well in school, had a job, and tried to help my family in everything I could. But the sadness never went away; it took so much of my energy. Most things and events young people my age enjoyed, I didn't. I tried, but always felt out of place, and felt it was a waste of my time and energy.

Finally, I graduated from high school and got a job as a secretary but soon felt it was not what I wanted to do. I then decided to go to beauty school and became a hairdresser. After 2 years, even though I was very successful and made good money, I felt I needed more, but couldn't figure out what. So, I went to business school to figure out if I wanted to be a businesswoman. After a couple of weeks, boredom was killing me! I had no idea what to do. And the depression and sadness was always with me — never left me. Then an angel came to rescue me and I was able to attend college on a full paid scholarship. I was 20 years old now. I attended a summer program in 1969, then continued to the next semester. I was finally feeling a little better, wishing this would last and I wouldn't drop out. Then on April 1, I was at a party in college, not really interested in anyone there. But I saw this guy whom I had seen on campus since January staring at me. He was a transfer student from Fresno. The party went on. He didn't approach me as I seemed unapproachable to him. I went home with a friend around 1 or 2 am. When I walked into my apartment, that guy was sitting in our dining room table! He was waiting for his friend who was very cozy with my roommate; they were using my sofa bed, so I had to sit there with this guy and wait till his friend and my roommate finished their smooching. By 7 am, we had talked, listening to Smoke Gets in Your Eyes all those hours. He told me his whole life story without holding back, which really moved me! And he asked me to be his wife! I thought he was crazy, not drunk, because we weren't drinking at all. I sarcastically answered, "Sure." But to him, it was a "Yes, I will marry you." The next week, this guy reserved the party house on campus for (Cinco de Mayo) May 5 for our wedding reception! I didn't know it though.

Soon, my professors were congratulating me; I had no idea why. Did I get another scholarship? Was I the star student with best grades? I finally asked one of my professors why I was being congratulated. He answered that that guy, Peter, had told everyone we were getting married!! I couldn't believe it and when I confronted him, he said that I had said "sure" when he proposed! I told him I was being sarcastic. He was very hurt, but told me he was very serious, that he loved me and couldn't think of living without me. He pleaded for us to please continue our relationship, got on his knees, and cried for my love! I never felt more loved or wanted in my whole life. I knew I liked him, too, and decided to give him another chance. We continued together, seeing each other every day on and off campus. He always made sure I ate, cooked for me at my apartment, or got me food from his dorm cafeteria. I also took him to meet my parents after a couple of weeks. My mom absolutely loved him right away! My dad, not at all. He was not happy with my choice of a guy!

CHAPTER 2

Finally, the semester was over, and we were going our own way; he was going to Fresno for the summer. I was going to work with my family in the fields in Lodi, Ca.

The day came when we got on the road to Lodi from LA; I was with my dear cousin, Ema, and her dad on a long day's drive. My cousin and I exchanged stories about who we were dating; I told her about Peter and how we were just dating, but wasn't sure how serious it was. Finally, we got to the labor camp in Lodi, around 6 pm, where we stayed every summer while we worked in the fields. As we entered the camp, I saw a car parked at the back, and thought I saw the guy from college sitting on the car's trunk! But I immediately convinced myself it wasn't possible. How could it be when I never told him exactly where I was going to be that summer? Or did I mention it to him? Anyway, the closer we got to the car, the more it looked like him! Oh my God, it was him! When my uncle stopped the car, Peter walked to the car, opened my door, and helped me out of the car. I was a mess, my lips were swollen from eating so many sunflower seeds, I had no shoes on, and my clothes were just rags. As I was getting out of the car, I was stuttering, asking why he was there. When did he get there? How did he know I would be there that day? He just smiled as he was helping me out of the car, and told me he had come for me! He asked if we could go to dinner. I said I would have to take a shower and get dressed. He said to take my time, that he would wait. As I was in the shower, I was feeling overwhelmed with so many emotions all at once — nervous, excited, confused, happy, scared. Once I got ready, we went into the city and he took me to a Chinese restaurant by the lake. He told me he had been waiting for me since 10 am, had met many of my relatives, and told them he was my fiancée! What?! I asked why he did that, and he answered that he wanted to marry me that summer before going back to college! I told him it was too soon, that we had just met in April. This was June. I also asked what he was going to do that summer. He answered he got a job in minicorps, as a teacher's assistant, only an hour from the labor camp! So, our summer experience was him coming every Friday and sleeping in his car, as my dad didn't want him to stay with us in our big tent. Every Friday, he brought me a present — a dress — another Friday, a pair of shoes, a piece of jewelry, etc. And he had even bought matching wedding bands! Not sure how he did it as he didn't have much money. Throughout the summer, he had to go with my family on weekends to work in the fields; my dad said that guy had to prove to him he was a man!

CHAPTER 3

The summer was going by fast. This guy was relentless in asking me to marry him every weekend without stopping. He pleaded with my mom to convince me to marry him. Of course, she loved him and told me he was born for me; she was convinced he would make me happy forever. She said she could see the love in his eyes for me. Finally, on August 26, I said ok! He was the happiest man on earth with my answer. The next day, we went downtown to get our marriage license. On August 28, my dad and mom went with us as our witnesses. My dad was furious — looked like he was going to pass out any minute; his jaws were clenched. My mom, on the other hand, was smiling and crying with joy.

Right after the ceremony at the courthouse, we got on a greyhound to Fresno, and when we got on the bus, we couldn't sit together since there were no 2 empty seats next to each other. An African American woman asked me where I was going. I said to Fresno. I also told her I had just gotten married before getting on the bus and that my new husband was sitting on the back of the bus. She said we had to sit together and volunteered to exchange places with my new husband. Of course, she announced it loudly and everyone on the bus were applauding the newlyweds. When we got to Fresno, my new in-laws made us a pork-chops dinner with beans and homemade tortillas. And in our wedding night, we shared a bedroom with 4 of my husband's sisters. They were a family of 12 and most of them still lived at home. The next day, bright and early, we went to work in the grapevines. I got stung by a wasp; I looked like a unicorn on my honeymoon in the grapevines! We worked like mad for a couple of weeks in the grapevines; we needed to buy a car to get back to college. Finally, we had enough money to buy our used car.

CHAPTER 4

Our journey as a married couple had begun!

Once back in college, we rented a shabby, furnished studio close to campus. The only furniture we had was a small TV, from me, and a typewriter from my new husband. So we had to buy our dishes and other necessary items from goodwill. Not sure why, but I felt happy, fulfilled, and so loved by that guy who was born for me. We both got 2 jobs, one in the morning as teacher aides at the high schools, and another as tutors at the university. We took all our classes in the evenings from 5 to 10 pm. Our days started at 7:30 each morning, and we finally got home around 10:30 pm. I did all the typing and editing for both of us; he did all the cooking and cleaning. This was our life for the next 3 years; work, go to school, study hard to pass our classes with good grades. We were newlyweds and really had no time to think about anything except work and school. Yet, we were extremely happy; we were so young, energetic, and focused for the future. And so in love with each other.

Those 3 years went by very fast; now we were graduating with our bachelor's degree. It was summer 1973. By the way, my dad had changed his feelings for my husband; he respected him now and even thanked him for accomplishing so much and making me so happy.

In our next journey, we applied to Teacher Corps; we wanted to be teachers and got accepted. We had to move to Salinas in Northern California where we did our teaching internship. We were interns at the high school. That year was very challenging because we had to teach, and also got very involved with many projects in the community. When that school year ended, I was offered a job at the school where I did my internship. But my husband didn't find a job and did substitute teaching. He felt like a failure and at the end of that school year, decided to travel south until he found a job. I stayed in Salinas since one of us had to hold a job. It was so incredibly hard to be away from each other, but we had no choice. That was the most difficult year of our marriage. He finally got a job in Santa Maria, California. We hated being apart. But we saw each other every weekend. Some weekends, he would come to see me; other weekends, I would go to see him. Then something wonderful happened. I got pregnant with our first baby! It was 1976. At the end of the school year, he came home, got a job near Salinas, and we bought our first home! When our baby was born, we were over the moon happy, but also overwhelmed and terrified. We both came from families of 12 and 10 children, but being responsible for our own baby was totally different. We tried our very best to be good parents and we were a happy little family. My mom was right; this man made me so happy, and I knew he was born for me!

The following few years were busy, happy, and fulfilling but our little girl was lonely; I was asked and pleaded to by my husband and my parents to give my little one a sibling. And in 1981, we were blessed with our beautiful second baby girl. Finally, our first born had a little sister and we were all filled with happiness and our joy grew so much. We felt so blessed.

CHAPTER 5

Then in 1985, we made a big decision to leave Salinas after 12 years and move to San Diego — a place I had wanted to move to for many years. It was quite a big move: a new city, new jobs, new big house, and we were expecting our third baby! This time, I decided to have our third baby. I felt we needed another baby to complete our family. When that beautiful baby came into our lives, we were crazy in love with her; now we were complete.

As far as moving to San Diego, we soon found out how beautiful San Diego was, and how lucky we were to finally live in that beautiful city. Our lives in San Diego were busy with our jobs and our three little girls.

CHAPTER 6

Through the years, our little girls growing to adolescents and young adults was a vision of beauty and it was sometimes challenging, too, especially when they were teenagers. But as long as we stuck together, we got through everything and in the end, felt closer. Of course, that man, who was born for me, did whatever it took to keep our family happy and together. Very soon, our daughters started living their own lives, getting married and blessing us with beautiful adorable grandchildren — our biggest blessings in our lives. Now, 53 years later, our grandkids are in college and high school, a couple in elementary school. As their grandparents, we live for them, cherish every minute we can spend together. We know how blessed we are to be living close to all of them and enjoying our golden years, thankful to be all together. And still I am grateful and thankful to be with that man who was born for me. And we're as in love as in 1970 — maybe even more!

CHAPTER 7

Now, both of us in our mid 70's are so incredibly grateful and thankful for all the beautiful people who love us and make our daily lives so full. Our three beautiful and strong daughters are also now super moms and wives, too. We named our first born Iris which means a beautiful flower and rainbow. Our second born, is Alba — meaning a beautiful new day. Our third born whom we named Aura is indeed the glow (and essence around a person). We chose these names because they are beautiful and fitting for each one of them. We hope we have been good role models to them throughout their childhood, adolescence, and adulthood. They are everything to us, our reason for being! Our biggest happiness today is to be with our 5 beautiful grandbabies: Sofia, our first granddaughter, so beautiful and brilliant; our only grandson, Lucas, so handsome and smart and sweet, who's our prince; our third granddaughter, Eva, incredibly sweet and smart and also beautiful; our fourth granddaughter, Bella, her name totally describes her — beautiful, and also smart and sweet; our littlest granddaughter, Isabel, we call her the littlest and beautiful princess because that is what she is to us. Yes, we are over the top parents and grandparents and give no apologies!

CHAPTER 8

After over 53 years of marriage, we are not going to say that everything has been wonderful and blissful because we've also had many challenges, rough times, incredible grief with the loss of dear ones, which have had a deep impact on our lives. And at times, they have made it very hard to see and feel the sunshine. But despite all these things, because our love is so true and strong, we have held on to all the good, positive things in our lives, above all, to all the incredible love from our children, our grandchildren, siblings, extended family, and dear friends. After 53-plus years of marriage, if we were to give any advice to anyone, it would be to always count your blessings, especially on difficult days, close your eyes and go back to the beginning of your life together, and feel what you both felt and keep that feeling with you. Remember the joy, the sudden feelings of incredible love you felt for each other. And that will carry you to the rest of your lives. We are grateful and so blessed to all of you for making our lives so special 🙌 🙏 We're looking forward to many more beautiful anniversaries 💝 🖤

www.ingramcontent.com/pod-product-compliance
Lightning Source LLC
LaVergne TN
LVHW020416070526
838199LV00054B/3639